Jordan Blake

Mastering Email Marketing

"Within the pixels of an email lies the power to captivate, connect, and convert. 'Mastering Email Marketing in 2023' is your guide to unlocking this potential, where each message becomes a brushstroke in the artistry of digital communication." - Jordan Blake

Jordan Blake

Contents

1.

2.

3.

4.

5.

6.

7.

8.

9.

10.

11.

12.

Foreword

Foreword by Jordan Blake

In the vast realm of digital communication, where attention is a prized commodity and connection is the currency, email marketing stands as a beacon of opportunity. As we delve into the pages of "Mastering Email Marketing in 2023," we embark on a journey that transcends conventional approaches, exploring the ever-evolving strategies that breathe life into your campaigns.

In this dynamic landscape, personalization isn't just a feature; it's a cornerstone. It's about understanding the heartbeat of your audience, anticipating their needs, and crafting messages that resonate on a personal level. As we navigate the intricacies of personalization within these pages, remember that every email holds the potential to be a conversation starter, a relationship builder.

But mastery extends beyond engagement—it embraces responsibility. Compliance isn't a mere checkbox; it's a commitment to respecting the trust bestowed upon us by our audience. It's about safeguarding data with vigilance and ensuring that every email sent is not just a message but a testament to ethical marketing practices.

As you immerse yourself in the strategies and insights shared in this guide, envision each chapter as a stepping stone toward a heightened understanding of the email marketing landscape. From the artistry of subject lines to the science of analyzing metrics, this guide is your compass in a landscape where relevance and resonance reign supreme.

Here's to embracing the transformative power of email marketing, where every click is a connection and every open is an opportunity. Let the journey begin.

Jordan Blake

Digital   Marketing   Explorer

Preface

Preface by Jordan Blake

Welcome to the dynamic world of email marketing, where the art of connection meets the science of strategy. In "Mastering Email Marketing in 2023," we embark on a journey to unravel the intricacies of crafting compelling campaigns that resonate with your audience and drive meaningful engagement.

As the digital landscape evolves, so do the tactics that captivate and convert. In this guide, we dive deep into the nuances of effective email marketing, exploring everything from the power of personalization to the critical importance of compliance in today's data-driven age.

Drawing upon years of experience in the ever-evolving realm of digital communication, I invite you to explore the strategies, techniques, and insights that can elevate your email marketing game. Whether you're a seasoned marketer seeking to refine your approach or a newcomer eager to harness the potential of this versatile tool, this guide is designed to empower you.

So, let's embark on this transformative journey together. From optimizing mobile experiences to decoding the latest trends, "Mastering Email Marketing in 2023" is your compass in navigating the evolving landscape of digital communication. Here's to crafting emails that not only land in inboxes but leave a lasting impact on the hearts and minds of your audience.

Jordan Blake

    Digital   Marketing   Enthusiast

Acknowledgement

Acknowledgment by Jordan Blake

In the vibrant tapestry of "Mastering Email Marketing in 2023," the realization of this endeavor has been a collective journey fueled by inspiration, collaboration, and unwavering dedication. As I reflect on the creation of this guide, I am profoundly grateful for the contributions of many remarkable individuals who have made this exploration into the heart of email marketing possible.

To the tireless team who lent their expertise, creativity, and passion, thank you for bringing each chapter to life with a shared commitment to excellence. Your dedication has transformed ideas into actionable insights and has shaped this guide into a comprehensive resource for marketers navigating the ever-changing landscape of digital communication.

I extend my appreciation to the mentors and industry leaders whose wisdom has guided not only my journey but has also enriched the content within these pages. Your invaluable contributions have added depth to the insights shared, making this guide a testament to the collective knowledge of our community.

To the readers and practitioners, thank you for your curiosity and commitment to mastering the art and science of email marketing. It is your engagement, enthusiasm, and thirst for knowledge that propels the evolution of our field.

In the spirit of continuous learning and growth, I invite you to delve into the pages ahead. May this guide serve as a source of inspiration, empowerment, and strategic guidance in your pursuit of email marketing mastery.

With gratitude,

Jordan Blake
Author, "Mastering Email Marketing in 2023"

1

Building a Targeted Email List:

Building a Targeted Email List:

1. Define Your Target Audience: Clearly identify the demographics, interests, and behaviors of your ideal audience. This ensures you collect emails from individuals genuinely interested in your content or products.

2. Use Opt-In Forms: Place opt-in forms strategically on your website, blog, and social media platforms. Clearly communicate the value subscribers will receive by signing up.

3. Offer Incentives: Encourage sign-ups by providing incentives such as exclusive content, discounts, or downloadable resources. This adds perceived value to being part of your email list.

4. Utilize Social Media: Leverage your social media channels to promote your email sign-up. Run campaigns or contests that encourage followers to subscribe.

5. Host Webinars or Events: Collect emails through webinars or events related to your niche. Participants who engage with your content are more likely to subscribe.

6. Optimize Landing Pages: Ensure your landing pages are user-friendly and optimized for conversions. A clear call-to-action and minimal form fields can boost sign-up rates.

7. Partner with Others: Collaborate with other businesses or influencers in your industry to cross-promote email sign-ups. This can expand your reach to a wider yet relevant audience.

8. Promote Through Content: Include call-to-action buttons or links within your blog posts, articles, or other content, directing readers to subscribe to your email list.

9. Run Targeted Ads: Use online advertising platforms to target specific demographics interested in your niche. Create compelling ad copy that highlights the benefits of joining your email list.

10. Regularly Clean Your List: Periodically remove inactive or disengaged subscribers. A smaller, engaged list is more valuable than a large, unresponsive one and helps maintain email deliverability.

2

Segmenting Your Email List:

Segmenting Your Email List:

1. Understand Your Audience: Analyze your audience's characteristics, behaviors, and preferences. Identify key factors that differentiate segments, such as location, purchase history, or engagement level.

2. Use Demographic Data: Segment based on demographic information like age, gender, or job role. This helps tailor content to specific groups with distinct needs or interests.

3. Behavioral Segmentation: Consider how subscribers interact with your emails, website, or products. Create segments for frequent buyers, occasional visitors, or those who haven't engaged recently.

4. Purchase History: If applicable, segment based on past purchase behavior. Target loyal customers with exclusive offers or re-engage those who haven't made a purchase recently.

5. Geographic Segmentation: Tailor messages to different regions or time zones. This is especially important for businesses with a global audience.

6. Preferences and Interests: Gather data on subscriber preferences and interests. Customize content to match their preferences, increasing the likelihood of engagement.

7. Engagement Levels: Identify highly engaged subscribers and those who need reactivation. Adjust your email frequency or content strategy accordingly.

8. Lifecycle Stage: Segment based on where subscribers are in their customer journey – new leads, active customers, or lapsed users. Provide relevant content to move them through the sales funnel.

9. Survey Your Audience: Use surveys to collect additional information directly from your subscribers. This can help create more nuanced segments and improve personalization.

10. Dynamic Content: Implement dynamic content in emails, allowing different content to be displayed based on the recipient's characteristics. This ensures a more personalized experience for 12 each segment.

3

Creating Compelling Content for Email Marketing:

Creating Compelling Content for Email Marketing:

1. Know Your Audience: Understand the interests, preferences, and pain points of your audience. Tailor your content to address their needs and provide value.

2. Craft a Clear Message: Clearly communicate your message. Use concise language and a compelling narrative to keep readers engaged.

3. Eye-Catching Subject Lines: Capture attention with captivating subject lines. Make it concise, intriguing, and relevant to the content of the email.

4. Personalization: Address subscribers by their names and use data to personalize content. This makes your emails feel more tailored to individual recipients.

5. Use Engaging Visuals: Incorporate images, infographics, or videos to make your emails visually appealing. Visual content is more likely to grab attention than plain text.

6. Mobile Optimization: Design emails with mobile users in mind. Ensure that your content is easily readable on various devices, considering different screen sizes.

7. Focus on Benefits: Clearly highlight the benefits of your product or service. Explain how it solves a problem or fulfills a need for the recipient.

8. Create a Call-to-Action (CTA): Clearly instruct readers on what action to take next. Whether it's making a purchase, signing up, or downloading, your CTA should be compelling and easily accessible.

9. Segmented Content: Tailor content based on audience segments. Provide different content to new subscribers, loyal customers, or those who haven't engaged in a while.

10. Testing and Optimization: A/B test different elements of your emails, such as subject lines, content, or CTA buttons. Analyze the results and optimize future emails based on what performs best.

Remember, the key is to provide value, build a connection with your audience, and make your emails a rewarding experience for recipients.

4

Optimizing Emails for Mobile:

Optimizing Emails for Mobile:

1. Responsive Design: Ensure your email design is responsive, meaning it adapts to different screen sizes. This guarantees a seamless and visually appealing experience on both smartphones and tablets.

2. Single-Column Layouts: Use a single-column layout to make your content easily scannable. This format accommodates the narrow width of mobile screens.

3. Large and Readable Fonts: Choose fonts that are easy to read on smaller screens. Use a font size of at least 14px for the body text to enhance readability.

4. Clickable Buttons: Design clear and clickable buttons. They should be large enough to tap without accidentally

clicking nearby elements, and include a compelling call-to-action.

5. Optimized Images: Compress images to reduce file size without compromising quality. Large image files can slow down load times, especially on mobile networks.

6. Preview Text: Craft engaging preview text that complements your subject line. This is often displayed in the inbox and can influence whether the recipient opens the email.

7. Minimize Text and Use Bullets: Keep your content concise. Use bullets and short paragraphs to break up text, making it easier for users to digest information quickly.

8. Test Across Devices: Test your emails on various devices and email clients to ensure consistent rendering. What looks good on one platform might appear differently on another.

9. Avoid Flashy Animations: Flashy animations or elements that rely on hover effects may not work well on mobile. Stick to elements that are supported across different devices.

10. Unsubscribe Link Accessibility: Ensure that the unsubscribe link is easily accessible. This not only complies

with regulations but also provides a positive user experience for those who wish to opt out.

5

Crafting Attention-Grabbing Subject Lines:

Crafting Attention-Grabbing Subject Lines:

1. Be Concise: Keep subject lines short and to the point. Aim for around 41-50 characters, as many email clients display a limited number of characters.

2. Create Urgency: Use language that conveys urgency without being overly aggressive. Limited-time offers or exclusive deals can motivate recipients to open your email quickly.

3. Ask Questions: Pose intriguing questions that spark curiosity. Encouraging recipients to seek answers can prompt them to open your email.

4. Use Numbers and Emojis Sparingly: Incorporate numbers or emojis for visual appeal, but use them sparingly. Too many can make your subject line appear cluttered.

5. Personalization: Include the recipient's name or reference their preferences when relevant. Personalized subject lines can make emails feel more tailored and increase open rates.

6. Highlight Benefits: Clearly communicate the value or benefit of opening the email. What will recipients gain or learn by engaging with your content?

7. Avoid Spam Triggers: Steer clear of all caps, excessive exclamation marks, or trigger words commonly associated with spam. These can lead to your emails being filtered out.

8. Test Different Approaches: Conduct A/B testing with variations of subject lines. Analyze which styles resonate best with your audience and adjust your strategy accordingly.

9. Segmented Messaging: Tailor subject lines based on audience segments. Different groups may respond better to varied tones or types of messaging.

10. Stay True to Content: Ensure your subject line aligns with the actual content of your email. Misleading subject

lines can lead to frustration and decreased trust from your audience.

21

6

Timing Matters:

Timing Matters:

1. *Know Your Audience's Habits: Understand the behavior and preferences of your target audience. When are they most likely to check their emails? Consider time zones if your audience is global.

2. A/B Test Send Times: Experiment with different send times and days of the week. A/B testing allows you to analyze which timing generates the best open and click-through rates.

3. Consider Industry Norms: Research and understand general industry trends regarding email engagement times. While it's essential to know your audience, industry benchmarks can provide valuable insights.

4. Mobile Usage Patterns: Take into account when your audience is most active on mobile devices. Many people check emails on their smartphones, so optimal send times may coincide with mobile usage peaks.

5. Avoid Busy Periods: Try to avoid sending emails during peak hours when people are inundated with messages. Off-peak times might result in less competition for attention.

6. Relevance to Content: Match the timing of your emails with the content. For instance, if you're promoting a lunchtime special, sending the email shortly before lunch can be more effective.

7. Dayparting: Divide the day into segments (dayparting) and analyze when engagement is highest. This method allows you to target specific time slots for different types of content or promotions.

8. Consider Work Hours: For B2B emails, consider sending during typical work hours. Professionals might be more receptive to business-related content during their workday.

9. Holiday and Event Timing: Align your email campaigns with holidays or events relevant to your audience. However, be mindful of increased competition during peak seasons.

24

10. Monitor Open Rates: Regularly monitor your email open rates over time to identify patterns. Adjust your sending schedule based on the historical performance of your campaigns.

7

Personalizing Your Emails:

Personalizing Your Emails:

1. Collect Relevant Data: Gather information about your subscribers beyond just their email addresses. This can include preferences, purchase history, or any other data that can enhance personalization.

2. Segment Your Audience:Divide your email list into segments based on shared characteristics. This allows you to tailor content and offers to specific groups, increasing relevance.

3. Dynamic Content: Utilize dynamic content in your emails, allowing different elements to be displayed based on the recipient's characteristics. This ensures a personalized experience for each subscriber.

4. Use Recipient's Name: Address your subscribers by their names. Personalizing the greeting creates a sense of connection and demonstrates that the email is intended specifically for them.

5. Recommendations Based on Behavior: Provide product or content recommendations based on the recipient's past behavior. If they've purchased or engaged with certain types of content, offer similar items.

6. Location-Based Personalization: Tailor your content or promotions based on the recipient's location. This can include regional offers or information relevant to their geographic area.

7. Lifecycle Stage Personalization: Adjust your messaging based on where subscribers are in their customer journey. New leads may receive different content than long-time customers or those at risk of churning.

8. Preference Center: Allow subscribers to customize their preferences through a preference center. This empowers them to choose the type and frequency of content they receive.

9. Personalized Subject Lines: Extend personalization to your subject lines. Incorporate the recipient's name or reference their preferences to capture their attention.

27

10. Feedback Surveys: Use feedback surveys to gather insights directly from your subscribers. This information can guide future personalization efforts and improve the overall customer   experience.

8

A/B Testing for Email Marketing:

A/B Testing for Email Marketing:

1. Define Clear Objectives: Clearly outline the goals of your A/B tests. Whether it's improving open rates, click-through rates, or conversion rates, having defined objectives is crucial.

2. Test One Element at a Time: To pinpoint the factors influencing your results, test one variable at a time. This could be subject lines, CTAs, images, or the timing of your emails.

3. Audience Segmentation: If applicable, segment your audience for A/B testing. Different segments may respond differently to variations, allowing for more nuanced insights.

4. Randomized Samples: Ensure your A/B test samples are randomized to eliminate bias. This helps in drawing accurate conclusions about the impact of changes.

5. Test with a Significant Sample Size: Use a sample size that is statistically significant. This ensures that the results are reliable and not due to random chance.

6. Test Across Various Segments: If your audience is diverse, conduct A/B tests across different segments to account for variations in preferences.

7. Consistent Timing: Keep the timing consistent when conducting A/B tests. Testing variations at different times might introduce confounding variables.

8. Monitor Relevant Metrics: Track key metrics such as open rates, click-through rates, and conversion rates. Analyzing these metrics provides insights into the impact of your changes.

9. Iterate Based on Results: Use the insights gained from A/B tests to refine your future email marketing strategies. Continuous iteration based on data-driven decisions is crucial for improvement.

10. Document and Learn: Keep a record of your A/B testing results. Documenting what works and what doesn't helps build a knowledge base for more effective future testing and optimization.

9

Monitoring and Analyzing Email Marketing Metrics:

Monitoring and Analyzing Email Marketing Metrics:

1. Open Rates: Track the percentage of recipients who open your emails. A high open rate indicates that your subject lines are effective and enticing.

2. Click-Through Rates (CTR): Measure the percentage of recipients who clicked on one or more links in your email. A higher CTR indicates that your content is engaging and relevant.

3. Conversion Rates: Monitor the percentage of recipients who took the desired action, such as making a purchase or filling out a form. Conversion rates help assess the effectiveness of your email in driving desired outcomes.

4. Bounce Rates: Keep an eye on bounce rates to identify delivery issues. High bounce rates may indicate problems with your email list quality or email deliverability.

5. Unsubscribe Rates: Track the number of subscribers who opt out of your email list. An increasing unsubscribe rate may signal that your content or frequency is not aligning with subscriber expectations.

6. Spam Complaints: Monitor the number of recipients marking your emails as spam. High spam complaint rates can harm your sender reputation and deliverability.

7. Device and Browser Analytics: Understand the devices and browsers your audience uses to open emails. Optimize your email design based on the most prevalent platforms.

8. Time-of-Day Analysis: Analyze the times of day when your emails perform best. This insight helps in optimizing the timing of your future campaigns for maximum impact.

9. Engagement Over Time: Track how engagement evolves over time. Identify patterns and trends to adapt your email marketing strategy to changing audience behaviors.

10. Return on Investment (ROI): Assess the overall impact of your email campaigns by measuring the return on investment. This involves evaluating the revenue generated compared to the costs associated with your email marketing efforts.

Regularly monitoring these metrics provides valuable insights into the effectiveness of your email marketing strategy, allowing you to make data-driven adjustments for continuous improvement.

10

Compliance with Email Marketing Regulations:

Compliance with Email Marketing Regulations:

1. Understand Regulations: Familiarize yourself with email marketing regulations such as GDPR, CAN-SPAM, and CASL, depending on your target audience. These regulations govern the collection, use, and protection of personal data.

2. Permission-Based Marketing: Ensure you have explicit consent from individuals before sending them marketing emails. Implement opt-in processes to collect consent, and avoid purchasing email lists.

3. Provide Unsubscribe Options: Include a clear and easy-to-find unsubscribe option in every email. Honor unsubscribe requests promptly to comply with regulations and maintain a positive sender reputation.

4. Include Physical Address: Include your physical business address in every email. This is a requirement under regulations like CAN-SPAM and adds transparency to your communications.

5. Data Security: Implement robust security measures to protect the personal data you collect. Encrypt sensitive information and regularly update security protocols to prevent unauthorized access.

6. Regular Compliance Audits: Conduct regular audits to ensure ongoing compliance with email marketing regulations. This includes reviewing your data collection practices, opt-in processes, and unsubscribe mechanisms.

7. Educate Your Team: Ensure that your marketing team is well-informed about email marketing regulations. Provide training to educate them on compliance requirements and best practices.

8. Third-Party Compliance: If you use third-party tools or services for email marketing, verify that they also adhere to relevant regulations. Choose reputable providers with a strong commitment to data protection.

9. Record Keeping: Maintain records of consent, opt-in processes, and unsubscribe requests. This documentation serves as evidence of compliance in case of regulatory inquiries.

10. Stay Informed: Keep yourself updated on any changes or updates to email marketing regulations. Compliance requirements may evolve, and staying informed helps you adapt your strategies accordingly.